BRITTNEY GRINER

WNBA STAR

By Douglas Lynne

Book design by Jake Nordby
Cover design by Jake Nordby

Photographs ©: Ross D. Franklin/AP Images, cover, 1; Eric Gay/AP Images, 4, 7; Charlie Neibergall/AP Images, 8–9; Rod Aydelotte/AP Images, 10; Jessica Hill/AP Images, 13; Kamil Krzaczynski/AP Images, 15; Mark J. Terrill/AP Images, 16, 23; Evgenia Novozhenina/Pool Reuters/AP Images, 18; Matt York/AP Images, 21; Red Line Editorial, 22

Press Box Books, an imprint of Press Room Editions.

Library of Congress Control Number: 2023909016

ISBN
978-1-63494-757-2 (library bound)
978-1-63494-764-0 (paperback)
978-1-63494-777-0 (epub)
978-1-63494-771-8 (hosted ebook)

Distributed by North Star Editions, Inc.
2297 Waters Drive
Mendota Heights, MN 55120
www.northstareditions.com

Printed in the United States of America
102023

ABOUT THE AUTHOR

Douglas Lynne is a freelance writer. He spent many years working in the media, first in newspapers and later for online organizations, covering everything from breaking news to politics to entertainment to sports. He lives in Minneapolis, Minnesota.

TABLE OF CONTENTS

USA
8

1

BIG-GAME BRITTNEY

Standing 6-foot-9, Brittney Griner towered over most opponents. That was about to be a problem for Japan's undersized basketball team. Griner was a center for the United States. Her team had won its first five games at the 2020 Olympics in Tokyo, Japan. Now only the host country stood in the way of Team USA's seventh straight gold medal.

Griner drives toward the basket on her way to scoring two points for Team USA.

Griner pulled down the rebound on Japan's first shot. Then she blocked Japan's second shot attempt. But where she really shined was on offense. Two minutes into the game, Griner posted up her defender at the edge of the paint. Her teammate Breanna Stewart fed her a pass. Then, with a quick move, Griner created space for an easy basket.

GOING FOR GOLDS

Brittney Griner was a finalist for the 2012 US Olympic team while still in college. However, she decided to focus on school and family. Four years later, she won her first Olympic gold medal with Team USA. Griner also won golds at the 2014 and 2018 FIBA Women's Basketball World Cups.

As the game went on, teammates kept passing Griner the ball under the basket. And she kept scoring. She put up 30 points in the 90–75 win. No woman had ever scored more points in an Olympic gold-medal game. Griner did it while making 14 of 18 shots.

Griner (15) celebrates with her teammate Sylvia Fowles (13) after beating Japan.

Griner holds up two fingers to tell fans it is her second Olympic gold medal.

Griner wasn't often in the spotlight during these Olympics. Two of her veteran teammates, Sue Bird and Diana Taurasi, had received most

of the attention in Tokyo. But when it was time to step up, Griner was ready.

"She's the ultimate teammate," Taurasi said after the game. "She'll do anything it takes for a team to win."

BAYLOR
42

BASKETBALL SUPERSTAR

2

Britney Griner was born on October 18, 1990, in Houston, Texas. From a young age, she was taller than her peers. They sometimes picked on her. Brittney later used those taunts as motivation to become a better athlete.

Brittney didn't start playing basketball until high school. But before long, she was a star. In one game, she blocked 25 shots. In another game, she dunked seven times.

Griner was only the seventh woman ever to dunk in a college basketball game.

Her Nimitz High team was one of the best in Texas. Most experts agreed Brittney was the top high school player in the country.

Every college team wanted her. Griner picked Baylor University in Waco, Texas. Baylor already had a good team. Griner quickly helped the Lady Bears become great. Early on, Griner stood out, especially on defense. By her junior year in 2011–12, she was the nation's best college player. The season ended with Griner cutting down the nets as a national champion.

The Phoenix Mercury had the top pick in the 2013 Women's National Basketball Association (WNBA) Draft. They picked Griner. She was named a WNBA All-Star as a rookie. The Mercury also went from one of the WNBA's worst teams to a winning team. And by 2014,

Griner shakes hands with WNBA President Laurel J. Richie after being drafted by Phoenix.

Phoenix was the WNBA champion. However, Griner missed the final game with an eye injury.

Griner proved that she was an elite player. She was a force under the basket, and she regularly led the league in blocks. In 2014 and 2015, Griner was the league's Defensive Player of the Year. Then, in 2017, she led the WNBA in scoring.

Two years later, Griner won a second WNBA scoring title. The Phoenix Mercury were a regular playoff team. Griner also won her second Olympic gold medal at the 2020 Olympics in Tokyo, Japan. She had become a superstar.

COMING OUT

Ahead of her WNBA debut, Brittney Griner came out publicly as gay. Few well-known athletes were out at the time. Griner said she hoped her example could help others. Many people supported Griner. She became the first openly gay athlete to sign an endorsement deal with Nike.

Griner lifts the WNBA championship trophy as she celebrates with teammate Diana Taurasi.

LifeLock
42
boost
mobile
10

3

DARK DAYS

WNBA players make far less money than male basketball players. To earn more, many WNBA players go overseas during the offseason. Griner played briefly in China. Starting in 2014, she began playing for a team in Russia.

In February 2022, Griner was traveling to meet her Russian team. She was arrested at an airport near Moscow. Local officials said she was bringing illegal

Griner ranks among the top 30 in total points scored in WNBA history.

Griner was going to spend nine years in a Russian prison, but the US government helped her get out.

drugs into the country. The US government investigated the arrest. It declared that Griner was "wrongfully detained," or should not be in jail.

A week later, Russia invaded the neighboring country of Ukraine. After that, people had trouble getting information from within Russia. Many worked hard to help Griner, including the US government. Progress was slow, however. Griner wrote that she was scared she might never get out. Finally, in December, the United States and Russia struck a deal. Russia released Griner. In exchange, the United States released a Russian prisoner.

HOME SUPPORT

Brittney Griner made her seventh WNBA All-Star Team in 2021. The league named her an honorary All-Star in 2022. Griner was still being held in Russia. But all the players wore her No. 42. It was one of many examples of the basketball community supporting Griner.

It was an emotional experience for Griner. She said she planned to play basketball again. But first, she wanted to spend some quiet time with her wife, Cherelle Griner.

In February 2023, fans got exciting news. The Mercury announced Griner was coming back for that year's WNBA season. "Today is a special day for all of us," a team official said.

BRITTNEY GRINER

WNBA CAREER STATISTICS (PER GAME)

- **2013** – 12.6 points, 6.3 rebounds, 3.0 blocks
- **2014** – 15.6 points, 8.0 rebounds, 3.8 blocks
- **2015** – 15.1 points, 8.1 rebounds, 4.0 blocks
- **2016** – 14.5 points, 6.5 rebounds, 3.1 blocks
- **2017** – 21.9 points, 7.6 rebounds, 2.5 blocks
- **2018** – 20.5 points, 7.7 rebounds, 2.6 blocks
- **2019** – 20.7 points, 7.2 rebounds, 2.0 blocks
- **2020** – 17.7 points, 7.5 rebounds, 1.8 blocks
- **2021** – 20.5 points, 9.5 rebounds, 1.9 blocks
- **2022** – did not play

Griner returned to the WNBA for the 2023 season.

TIMELINE MAP

1. **Houston, Texas: 1990**
   Brittney Griner is born on October 18.
2. **Waco, Texas: 2009**
   Griner begins her record-setting college career at Baylor University.
3. **Denver, Colorado: 2012**
   Griner records 26 points, 13 rebounds, and 5 blocks as Baylor wins the college national title. She is named the Most Outstanding Player at the Final Four.
4. **Phoenix, Arizona: 2013**
   Griner makes her WNBA debut for the Phoenix Mercury on May 27.
5. **Rio de Janeiro, Brazil: 2016**
   Griner makes her first appearance at the Olympics. She starts all eight games and helps Team USA win a gold medal.
6. **Tokyo, Japan: 2021**
   Griner's 30 points help Team USA win a seventh straight Olympic gold medal.
7. **Moscow, Russia: 2022**
   In February, Griner is arrested at an airport near the Russian capital. The US government later says she was wrongfully arrested. Griner is released in December.
8. **Los Angeles, California: 2023**
   On May 19, fans and players give Griner a warm welcome as she plays in her first game after being released.

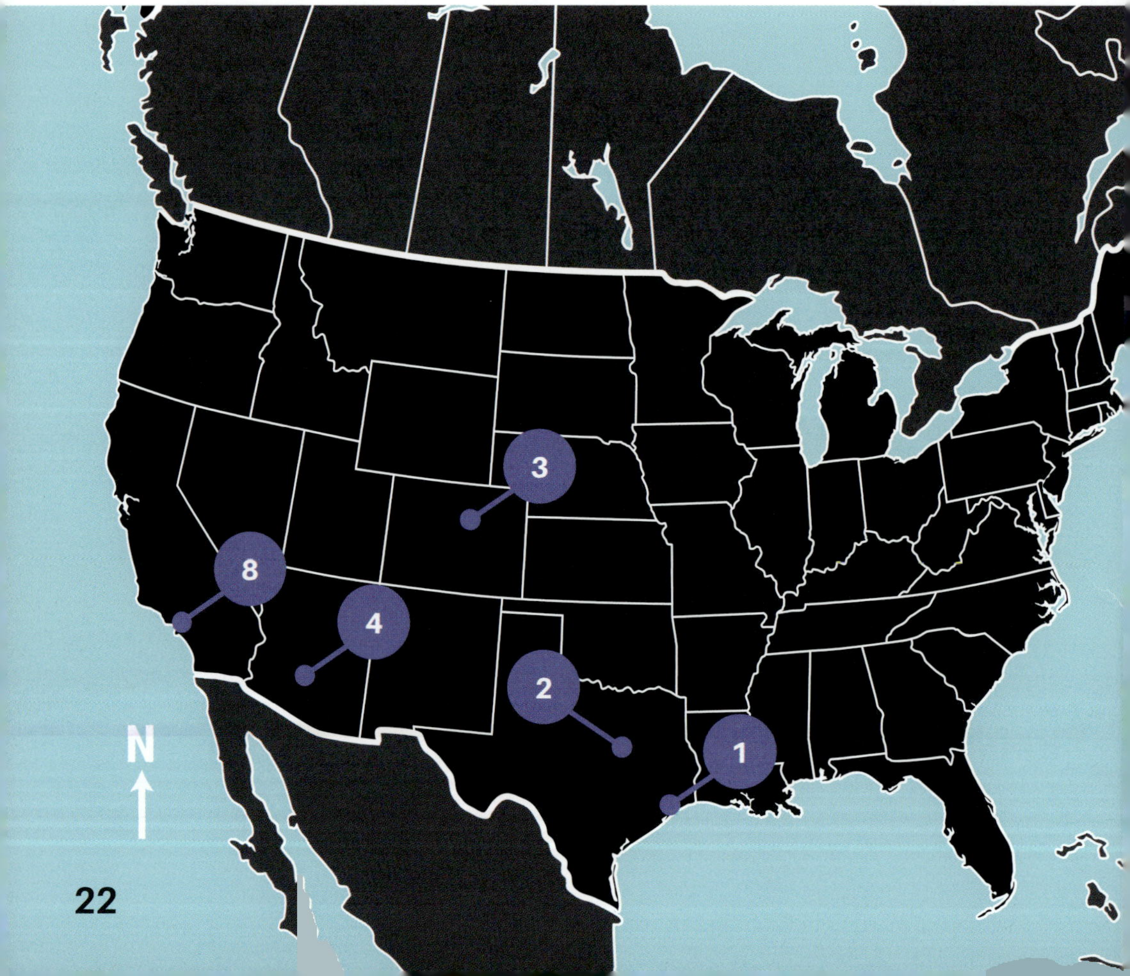

AT-A-GLANCE

BRITTNEY GRINER

Birth date: October 18, 1990

Birthplace: Houston, Texas

Position: Center

Height: 6 feet 9 inches

Weight: 205 pounds

Current team: Phoenix Mercury (2013–)

Past team: Baylor Lady Bears (2009–13)

Major awards: College National Player of the Year (2012, 2013), Final Four Most Outstanding Player (2012), WNBA All-Star (2013, 2014, 2015, 2017, 2018, 2019, 2021), WNBA Defensive Player of the Year (2014, 2015), First Team All-WNBA (2014, 2019, 2021)

Accurate through the 2022 season.

MORE INFORMATION

To learn more about Brittney Griner, go to **pressboxbooks.com/AllAccess**.

These links are routinely monitored and updated to provide the most current information available.

GLOSSARY

debut
First appearance.

draft
An event that allows teams to choose new players coming into a league.

endorsement
When a company pays someone to promote the company or its products.

honorary
Recognized despite not meeting the usual requirements.

paint
Another term for the lane, the area between the basket and the free throw line.

rookie
A first-year player.

veteran
A player who has spent several years in a league.

INDEX